The Ultimate UK Ninja Foodi Dual Zone Air Fryer Cookbook

1500 Days of Irresistible Air-Fried Delights Using the Metric Measurements and No-Fuss Local Ingredients to Excite Your Palate | Full Colour Edition

Lucy Simmons

Copyright© 2024 By Lucy Simmons Rights Reserved

This book is copyright protected. It is only for personal use. You cannot amend, distribute, sell, use, quote or paraphrase any part of the content within this book, without the consent of the author or publisher.

Under no circumstances will any blame or legal responsibility be held against the publisher, or author, for any damages, reparation, or monetary loss due to the information contained within this book, either directly or indirectly.

Disclaimer Notice:

Please note the information contained within this document is for educational and entertainment purposes only. All effort has been executed to present accurate, up to date, reliable, complete information. No warranties of any kind are declared or implied. Readers acknowledge that the author is not engaged in the rendering of legal, financial, medical or professional advice. The content within this book has been derived from various sources. Please consult a licensed professional before attempting any techniques outlined in this book.

By reading this document, the reader agrees that under no circumstances is the author responsible for any losses, direct or indirect, that are incurred as a result of the use of the information contained within this document, including, but not limited to, errors, omissions, or inaccuracies.

Editor: AALIYAH LYONS

Interior Design: BROOKE WHITE

Cover Art: DANIELLE REES

Food stylist: Sienna Adams

Table Of Contents

Introduction	1
Chapter 1	
Unveiling the Ninja Foodi Dual Zone Air Fryer	2
Features and Specifications	3
Air Fryer Cooking Chart	6
Chapter 2	
Breakfast and Brunch	8
Basic Breakfast Bread	9
Courgette Fritters	9
Healthy Spinach Egg Cups	10
Cheddar & Cream Omelet	10
Chicken Egg Muffins	11
Baked Breakfast Quiche	11
Hash Brown Egg Cups	12
Tropical Steel-Cut Oatmeal	12
Dutch Baby	13
Granola with Cashews	13
Red Shakshuka	14
Tuna Breakfast Muffins	14
Pancetta & Spinach Frittata	15
Sausage Bake Omelet	15
Chapter 3	
Snacks and Appetizer Recipes	16
Tofu Nuggets	17
Baked Mozzarella Sticks	17
Red Pepper Feta Dip	18
Onion Rings	18
Pumpkin Fries	19
Easy Corn Dip	19
Beef Taquitos	20
Cinnamon Sugar Pinwheels	20
Cheesy Broccoli Bites	21
Air Fryer Ravioli	21
Papas Bravas	22
Cherry Clafoutis	22
Chapter 4	
Beef, Pork and Lamb Recipes	23

Garlic Balsamic Lamb Chops	24
Garlicky Lamb Chops	24
Rump Steak	25
Flavorful Pork Patties	25
Meatloaf	26
Greek lamb Farfalle	26
Lamb and Vegetable Curry	27
Mustard Roasted Pork Tenderloin	27
Shepherd's Pie	28
Italian Sausages with Polenta and Grapes	28
Beef Short Ribs	29
Ravioli with Meat Sauce	29
Greek Pork Chops	30
Glazed Beef Short Ribs	30
Pork Fried Rice with Mushrooms and Peas	31
Beef Patties	31

Chapter 5
Poultry Recipes — **32**

Thanksgiving Turkey	33
Tasty Chicken Drumsticks	33
Chicken Tomato Mushrooms Bake	34
Chicken Casserole	34
Parmesan Chicken Tenders	35
Spicy Meatballs	35
Chicken and Mushroom Pie	36
Chicken Taquitos	36
Chicken Tikka Masala	37
Parmesan Crusted Chicken Breasts	37
Crispy Chicken Cutlets	38
Balsamic Chicken	38
Greek Chicken Casserole	39
Cheesy Chicken	39

Chapter 6
Fish and Seafood Recipes — **40**

Cod Parcel	41
Tuna Patties	41
Shrimp Scampi	42
Greek Shrimp	42
Honey Mustard Salmon with Asparagus	43
Basil Garlic Shrimp	43
Lobster Tail Casserole	44
Baked Tilapia with Buttery Crumb Topping	44
Teriyaki Salmon with Baby Bok Choy	45
Salmon & Asparagus Parcel	45
Seafood Casserole	46
Salmon Patties	46

Chapter 7
Vegetables and Sides Recipes — **47**

Succotash	48
Stuffed Peppers	49
Potato Casserole	49
Green Tomatoes	50
Vegetable Nachos	50
Black Bean Veggie Burgers	51
Roast Cauliflower and Broccoli	51
Japanese Curry	52
Quinoa Burgers	53
Orange and Saffron-Scented Rice Pilaf	53
Ham Hock Braised Greens	54
Beans & Veggie Burgers	54
Broccoli & Rice	55
Cumin and Orange-Maple-Glazed Carrots	55

Chapter 8
Dessert Recipes — **56**

Cinnamon Rolls	57
Nutella Brownies	57
Shortbread Fingers	58
Chocolate Chip Cookie	58
Banana Pancakes Dippers	59
Easy Carrot Cake	59
Cookie Cake	60
Cherry Crumble	60
Marinara Sauce	61
Brownie Muffins	61

Appendix 1 Measurement Conversion Chart	**62**
Appendix 2 The Dirty Dozen and Clean Fifteen	**63**
Appendix 3 Index	**64**

Introduction

In the ever-evolving landscape of modern cooking, where technology and innovation intersect with our love for delicious, home-cooked meals, kitchen appliances have become indispensable companions. At the forefront of this culinary revolution stands the Ninja Foodi Dual Zone Air Fryer – a versatile and efficient tool that has reshaped the way we approach home cooking. It is with great excitement that I introduce you to this collection of culinary delights, a cookbook that unveils the incredible potential of the Ninja Foodi Dual Zone Air Fryer.

within these pages lies more than just a compilation of recipes; it is a gateway to a new era of culinary exploration, where the limits of the kitchen are pushed, and the art of cooking is taken to new heights. Regardless of your skill level in the kitchen, the Ninja Foodi Dual Zone Air Fryer will become your trusted partner in the pursuit of mouthwatering and wholesome meals, and this cookbook is your guide to unlocking its full potential.

The recipes found here showcase a diverse array of dishes, thoughtfully crafted to cater to various tastes and dietary preferences. From achieving that perfect crispiness in air-fried classics to creating succulent roasts, indulgent desserts, and a spectrum of culinary delights, each recipe highlights the versatility of the Ninja Foodi Dual Zone Air Fryer. The dual-zone technology, allowing independent temperature control in two separate compartments, opens up a world of possibilities, enabling you to cook multiple dishes simultaneously with precision and perfection.

As you explore the recipes, you'll uncover the delicate balance of flavors, textures, and aromas that transform ordinary ingredients into extraordinary culinary creations. The Ninja Foodi Dual Zone Air Fryer's ability to air fry, roast, bake, and dehydrate empowers you to embrace healthier cooking methods without compromising on taste. It is a testament to how modern technology can enhance our culinary experiences, making every meal a celebration of creativity and nourishment.

Beyond the recipes, this cookbook serves as a comprehensive guide to mastering the intricacies of the Ninja Foodi Dual Zone Air Fryer. Detailed instructions, cooking tips, and insights into the appliance's features ensure that you can confidently navigate your way through each culinary endeavor. Whether you are a busy professional seeking quick and wholesome weekday meals or a passionate home cook eager to impress friends and family, this cookbook provides the inspiration and guidance you need.

Cooking is not merely a means of sustenance; it is a form of self-expression, an act of love, and a source of joy. This collection invites you to embark on a culinary adventure where the thrill of experimentation meets the satisfaction of creating memorable meals. As you explore the delicious possibilities within these pages, may your kitchen become a canvas, and the Ninja Foodi Dual Zone Air Fryer, your brush, painting a masterpiece of flavors that captivate the senses and nourish the soul.

I extend my warmest wishes to you, the reader, as you embark on this culinary journey. May your kitchen be filled with the enticing aromas and delightful sizzles of success as you embrace the art of cooking with the Ninja Foodi Dual Zone Air Fryer. Happy cooking!

Chapter 1

Unveiling the Ninja Foodi Dual Zone Air Fryer

Features and Specifications

In the bustling world of modern kitchens, where efficiency meets culinary finesse, the Ninja Foodi Dual Zone Air Fryer emerges as a game-changer, seamlessly blending innovation with practicality. As we delve into the features and specifications of this remarkable appliance, it becomes evident that every aspect is meticulously crafted to elevate your cooking experience.

DUAL-ZONE TECHNOLOGY

At the heart of the Ninja Foodi Dual Zone Air Fryer is its groundbreaking dual-zone technology. This feature allows for independent temperature control in two separate compartments, transforming the way we approach meal preparation. Imagine the convenience of air frying crispy chicken wings in one zone while simultaneously baking a delicate dessert in the other. This not only saves time but opens up a world of possibilities for creating multi-course meals with perfect timing.

SIX CUSTOMIZABLE COOKING FUNCTIONS

Versatility takes center stage with the Ninja Foodi Dual Zone Air Fryer, offering six distinct cooking functions – Air Fry, Roast, Bake, Reheat, Dehydrate, and Max Crisp. These functions are not mere buzzwords; they translate into real-world utility. Air Fry delivers guilt-free indulgence with less oil, while Roast and Bake cater to those seeking succulent roasts or perfectly baked goods. Reheat ensures leftovers taste as good as the first serving, and Dehydrate opens up a realm of possibilities for preserving fruits, vegetables, and even crafting homemade snacks. The Max Crisp function? It's the secret ingredient for achieving an irresistible crunch.

SMART FINISH FEATURE

Picture this: You're preparing a feast, and each dish requires a precise finishing touch. The Smart Finish feature anticipates this need, allowing you to program one zone to finish cooking before the other. This thoughtful addition ensures that every element of your meal is served at its absolute best, eliminating the challenge of coordinating different cooking times for various dishes.

EASY-TO-USE DIGITAL DISPLAY

Practicality meets user-friendly design with the Ninja Foodi Dual Zone Air Fryer's intuitive digital display. Say goodbye to guesswork as you navigate through temperature settings, cooking times, and functions with ease. The clear and concise interface empowers both beginners and seasoned cooks to harness the full potential of this appliance, making precision cooking accessible to all.

LARGE COOKING CAPACITY

The Ninja Foodi Dual Zone Air Fryer doesn't just cater to intimate family dinners; it's designed to handle larger gatherings with its generous cooking capacity. with the ability to cook up to 8-quarts of your favorite dishes, it effortlessly accommodates the diverse needs of households of all sizes, making it a practical and efficient choice for everyday cooking or entertaining guests.

DISHWASHER-SAFE ACCESSORIES

The convenience extends beyond cooking to the cleanup process. The accessories accompanying the Ninja Foodi Dual Zone Air Fryer – including the cooking baskets, crisper plates, and cooking pans – are all dishwasher-safe. This thoughtful feature ensures that the joy of a delicious meal is not followed by a tedious cleanup, making it a practical choice for those who value both efficiency and ease of maintenance in their kitchen appliances.

TIPS AND TRICKS FOR CULINARY SUCCESS

Embarking on a culinary journey with the Ninja Foodi Dual Zone Air Fryer is an exciting adventure, and like any journey, having a few expert tips and tricks up your sleeve can make all the difference. Let's dive into the practical insights that will elevate your cooking game and ensure a seamless and delicious experience.

PREHEAT WITH PURPOSE

Just like with traditional ovens, preheating your Ninja Foodi Dual Zone Air Fryer is key to achieving optimal results. This step ensures that your food cooks evenly and efficiently, especially crucial for recipes that rely on precise temperature control. Give your air fryer a head start, and you'll be rewarded with consistently delectable dishes.

MASTERING THE DUAL ZONES

Understanding the power of the dual-zone technology is essential. When cooking multiple dishes simultaneously, leverage the independent temperature control to tailor each zone to the specific needs of your recipes. This feature is a game-changer for creating well-coordinated, multi-course meals without the hassle of juggling multiple appliances or constantly checking on individual dishes.

EMBRACE THE AIR FRYER BASKET SHAKE

For recipes that require a thorough and even crisp, don't forget to shake the air fryer basket. Midway through the cooking process, give the basket a gentle shake to ensure that the ingredients are evenly exposed to the circulating hot air. This simple action can make a significant difference in achieving that perfect golden and crispy exterior.

CUSTOMIZE COOKING TIMES

While the Ninja Foodi Dual Zone Air Fryer comes with pre-set cooking times for various functions, it's essential to remember that individual preferences and ingredient sizes can vary. Get comfortable with customizing cooking times to suit your taste. Keep an eye on your creations, and when needed, adjust the cooking time for that ideal level of doneness.

EXPERIMENT WITH MARINADES AND RUBS

Enhance the flavor profile of your dishes by experimenting with marinades and rubs. The Ninja Foodi's ability to lock in flavors makes it the perfect canvas for infusing your favorite seasonings into meats, vegetables, and more. Give your ingredients a flavor boost by letting them marinate before cooking, or apply a dry rub for an added layer of taste and texture.

LAYERING FOR EFFICIENCY

When cooking multiple items that require different temperatures or cooking times, consider layering. Place quicker-cooking items on the top layer and those that require more time on the bottom. This clever strategy maximizes the use of both zones and ensures that each component is perfectly cooked.

DON'T FORGET ABOUT DEHYDRATION
Explore the dehydrate function beyond the realm of traditional snacks. Use it to preserve fruits, vegetables, and herbs or create your own homemade fruit leather. The Ninja Foodi Dual Zone Air Fryer's dehydrate function is a versatile tool for extending the shelf life of your favorite produce.

OPTIMAL AIR CIRCULATION
For optimal air circulation and even cooking, avoid overcrowding the cooking zones. Giving your ingredients enough space allows the hot air to circulate freely, ensuring that every nook and cranny receives the attention it deserves. It's a simple yet effective way to guarantee consistent and delightful results.

UTILIZE THE SMART FINISH FEATURE
When planning a multi-course meal, take advantage of the Smart Finish feature. Program one zone to finish cooking before the other, ensuring that each component is served at its prime. This thoughtful feature simplifies the coordination of diverse dishes, making you feel like a culinary maestro orchestrating a symphony of flavors.

KEEP IT CLEAN
A well-maintained kitchen appliance is a happy one. Regularly clean the accessories, baskets, and trays of your Ninja Foodi Dual Zone Air Fryer to prevent any buildup that may affect performance. The dishwasher-safe components make cleanup a breeze, ensuring that your air fryer is always ready for the next culinary masterpiece.

Armed with these practical tips and tricks, your culinary journey with the Ninja Foodi Dual Zone Air Fryer is destined for success. May your kitchen be filled with the delicious aromas of experimentation and your table adorned with culinary masterpieces. Happy cooking!

Air Fryer Cooking Chart

Food	Temperature (°C)	Cooking Time (minutes)
French fries (thin)	200	10-15
French fries (thick)	200	15-20
Chicken wings	180	20-25
Chicken breast	180	15-20
Salmon fillet	200	8-10
Shrimp	200	8-10
Onion rings	200	8-10
Vegetables (broccoli, etc.)	180	10-15
Frozen vegetables (mix)	180	10-15
Breaded fish fillets	200	10-12
Hamburgers	200	8-10
Bacon	180	6-8
Sausages	180	12-15
Meatballs	180	12-15
Baked potatoes	200	45-50
Sweet potatoes	200	20-25
Chicken breasts	200	15-20 min
Chicken thighs	200	20-25 min
Chicken wings	200	18-20 min
Fish fillets	200	8-12 min
Shrimp	200	6-8 min
Scallops	200	6-8 min
Salmon	200	10-12 min
Pork chops	200	12-15 min
Pork tenderloin	200	20-25 min
Steak (1 inch thick)	200	8-10 min
Hamburger patties	200	8-10 min
Hot dogs/sausages	200	6-8 min
French fries	200	15-20 min
Sweet potato fries	200	15-20 min
Potato wedges	200	15-20 min
Onion rings	200	12-15 min
Zucchini/squash fries	200	10-12 min
Broccoli/cauliflower	200	8-10 min
Brussel sprouts	200	12-15 min
Carrots	200	12-15 min

Food	Temperature (°C)	Cooking Time (minutes)
Asparagus	200	6-8 min
Corn on the cob	200	12-15 min
Baked potatoes	200	40-45 min
Stuffed mushrooms	200	8-10 min
Roasted peppers	200	8-10 min
Chicken nuggets	200	10-12 min
Meatballs	200	10-12 min
Spring rolls	200	10-12 min
Mozzarella sticks	200	6-8 min
Jalapeno poppers	200	8-10 min
Quiche	180	25-30 min
Puff pastry	200	10-12 min
Apple turnovers	200	12-15 min
Chocolate chip cookies	180	6-8 min

Note: Cooking times may vary depending on the type and brand of air fryer, as well as the size and thickness of the food being cooked. Always refer to the manufacturer's instructions and use a food thermometer to ensure that food is cooked to a safe temperature.

Chapter 2

Breakfast and Brunch

Basic Breakfast Bread

Prep time: 5 minutes | Cook time: 15 minutes | Serves 4

- 207ml whole-wheat flour
- 207ml plain flour
- 1 ¾ ounces pumpkin seeds
- 1 teaspoon salt
- ½ of sachet instant yeast
- ½-236ml lukewarm water

1. In a bowl, mix the flours, pumpkin seeds, salt, and yeast and mix well.
2. Slowly, add the desired amount of water and mix until a soft dough ball forms. with your hands, knead the dough until smooth and elastic.
3. Place the dough ball into a bowl. with plastic wrap, cover the bowl and set it aside in a warm place for 30 minutes or until doubled in size.
4. When cooking time is completed, open the door and place the pan onto a wire rack for about 10-15 minutes.
5. Carefully invert the bread onto the wire rack to cool completely cool before slicing.
6. Cut the bread into desired-sized slices and serve.

Courgette Fritters

Prep time: 15 minutes | Cook time: 7 minutes | Serves 4

- 300g courgette, grated and squeezed
- 255g Halloumi cheese
- 60g all-purpose flour
- 2 eggs
- 1 teaspoon fresh dill, minced
- salt and ground black pepper, as required

1. In a large bowl and mix all the ingredients together.
2. Make small-sized fritters from the mixture.
3. Press "Power" button of Ninja Foodi Digital Air Fry Oven and turn the dial to select "Air Fry" mode.
4. Press TIME/SLICE button and again turn the dial to set the cooking time to 7 minutes
5. Now push TEMP/DARKNESS button and rotate the dial to set the temperature at 170℃.
6. Arrange fritters into the greased sheet pan and insert in the oven.
7. When cooking time is completed, open the oven door and serve warm.

Healthy Spinach Egg Cups

Prep time: 5 minutes | **Cook time:** 20 minutes |Serves 6

- 6 egg
- 1/8 tsp onion powder
- 1/8 tsp garlic powder
- 79ml feta cheese, crumbled
- 354ml spinach, chopped
- Pepper
- Salt

1. Spray muffin pan with cooking spray and set aside.
2. Divide spinach and cheese evenly into each muffin cup.
3. In a bowl, whisk egg with onion powder, pepper, garlic powder, and salt.
4. Pour egg mixture into each cup.
5. Select bake then set the temperature to 176℃ and time to 20 minutes. Press start.
6. Once the oven is preheated then place the muffin pan into the oven.
7. Serve and enjoy.

Cheddar & Cream Omelet

Prep time: 5 minutes | **Cook time:** 8 minutes |Serves 2

- 4 egg
- 60g cream
- 1 teaspoon fresh parsley, minced
- Salt and ground black pepper, as required
- 60g Cheddar cheese, grated

1. In a bowl, add the egg, cream, parsley, salt, and black pepper and beat well.
2. Place the egg mixture into SearPlate.
3. Press AIR OVEN MODE button of Ninja Foodi Dual Heat Air Fry Oven and turn the dial to select "Air Fry" mode.
4. Press TIME/SLICES button and again turn the dial to set the cooking time to 8 minutes.
5. Press "Start/Stop" button to start.
6. When cooking time is completed, open the oven door and remove the SearPlate.
7. Cut the omelet into 2 portions and serve hot.

Chicken Egg Muffins

Prep time: 5 minutes | Cook time: 15 minutes |Serves 12

- 10 egg
- 450g parsley, chopped
- 15g Italian seasoning
- 236ml cooked chicken, chopped
- 1g garlic powder
- Pepper
- Salt

1. Place rack in the bottom position and close door. Select bake mode set the temperature to 204℃ and set the timer to 15 minutes. Press the setting dial to preheat.
2. In a large bowl, whisk egg with garlic powder, Italian seasoning, parsley, pepper, and salt.
3. Add remaining ingredients and stir well.
4. Pour egg mixture into the greased muffin pan.
5. Once the unit is preheated, open the door, and place the muffin pan onto the center of the rack, and close the door.
6. Serve and enjoy.

Baked Breakfast Quiche

Prep time: 5 minutes | Cook time: 55 minutes |Serves 6

- 8 egg
- 236ml sour cream
- 3/1.8kg ranch seasoning
- 354ml cheddar cheese, shredded
- 450g ground Italian sausage
- Pepper
- Salt

1. Brown the ground sausage in a pan over medium heat. Drain well and set aside.
2. In a large bowl, whisk egg with cream, ranch seasoning, pepper, and salt. Add sausage and cheese and stir well.
3. Pour egg mixture into the greased baking dish.
4. Select bake mode then set the temperature to 176℃ and time for 55 minutes. Press start.
5. Once the oven is preheated then place the baking dish into the oven.
6. Slice and serve.

Hash Brown Egg Cups

Prep time: 5 minutes | Cook time: 30 minutes | Serves 12

- 8 egg
- 60g milk
- 1g garlic powder
- 236ml ham, cubed
- 354ml cheddar cheese, grated
- 20 oz hash browns
- Salt

1. Spray muffin pan with cooking spray and set aside.
2. In a bowl, whisk egg with milk, pepper, and salt. Add ham, cheese, and hash browns and stir to combine.
3. Pour egg mixture into the greased muffin pan.
4. Select bake then set the temperature to 176℃ and time to 30 minutes. Press start.
5. Once the oven is preheated then place the muffin pan into the oven.
6. Serve and enjoy.

Tropical Steel-Cut Oatmeal

Prep time: 5 minutes | Cook time: 25 minutes | Serves 4

- 175 grams steel-cut oats
- 4 allspice berries
- 1/2 teaspoon kosher salt
- 120 ml whole milk or your favorite milk alternative
- 2 tablespoons light brown sugar

1. Place the oats, allspice, salt, and 400ml water into the Foodi's inner pot. Lock on the Pressure Lid, making sure the valve is set to Seal, and set to Pressure on High for 10 minutes. Turn off the Foodi and allow the pressure to release naturally for 15 minutes. Then quick-release any remaining pressure and carefully remove the lid.
2. Remove the allspice berries and stir in the milk and brown sugar. Divide among bowls and serve topped with fruit.

Dutch Baby

Prep time: 5 minutes | Cook time: 30 minutes | Serves 4

- 175 ml whole milk
- 3 large eggs
- 1 teaspoon vanilla extract
- 60 grams unsalted butter, melted
- 65 grams all-purpose flour
- 2 tablespoons cornstarch
- 1 tablespoon granulated sugar

1. In a medium bowl, vigorously whisk together the milk and eggs until frothy, about 1 minute. Add the vanilla and 28 grams of the butter, whisk, then add the flour, cornstarch, and granulated sugar, whisking until well combined, about 1 minute more.
2. Set the Foodi to Sear/Saute on High and preheat the Foodi for 5 minutes. Add the remaining 28 grams butter and stir it constantly until browned, about 6 minutes. At this point, the pancake will be set.
3. Lift the lid and carefully remove the inner pot from the Foodi. Run a silicone spatula around the edges of the pancake. Slide the Dutch Baby onto a plate and serve warm, topped with whipped cream, berries, and confectioners' sugar.

Granola with Cashews

Prep time: 5 Minutes | Cook time: 12 Minutes | Serves 6

- 300 grams old-fashioned rolled oats
- 200 grams raw cashews or mixed raw nuts (such as pecans, walnuts, almonds)
- 80 grams unsweetened coconut chips
- 120 ml honey
- 60 ml vegetable oil, extra-virgin olive oil, or walnut oil
- 70 grams packed light brown sugar
- 1/4 teaspoon kosher salt or 1/8 teaspoon fine salt

1. Place the oats, nuts, coconut, honey, oil, brown sugar, and salt in a large bowl and mix until well combined. Spread the mixture in an even layer on the sheet pan.
2. Once the unit has preheated, slide the pan into the oven.
3. After 5 to 6 minutes, remove the pan and stir the granola, return the pan to the oven, and continue cooking.
4. When cooking is complete, remove the pan. Let the granola cool to room temperature, then stir in the cranberries, if using. If not serving right away, store in an airtight container at room temperature.

Red Shakshuka

Prep time: 5 minutes | Cook time: 20 minutes | Serves 6

- 2 red bell peppers, seeded, ribbed, and diced
- 1/2 medium yellow onion, diced
- 15 ml tomato paste
- 1 (800 grams) can crushed tomatoes
- 30 ml Harissa (homemade or store-bought)
- 2 teaspoons ground cumin
- 60 ml olive oil
- 2.5 grams kosher salt
- 6 large eggs

1. Place the bell peppers, onion, garlic, tomato paste, crushed tomatoes, harissa, cumin, olive oil, and 120 ml water in the. When the timer reaches 0, quick-release the pressure and carefully remove the lid.
2. Crack 1 egg into a measuring cup, being careful not to break the yolk. Carefully pour the egg on top of the shakshuka. Repeat with the remaining eggs, spacing them evenly around the top.
3. Drop the Crisping Lid and set to Broil for 8 minutes, or until the whites are set. Serve immediately with pita or bread.

Tuna Breakfast Muffins

Prep time: 5 minutes | Cook time: 25 minutes | Serves 8

- 2 egg, lightly beaten
- 1 can tuna, flaked
- 59ml sour cream
- 59ml mayonnaise
- 30g cayenne
- 1 celery stalk, chopped
- 354ml mozzarella cheese, shredded
- Pepper
- Salt

1. Place rack in the bottom position and close door. Select bake mode set the temperature to 176℃ and set the timer to 25 minutes. Press the setting dial to preheat.
2. In a bowl, whisk egg with pepper and salt. Add remaining ingredients and stir well.
3. Pour egg mixture into the greased muffin pan.
4. Once the unit is preheated, open the door, and place the muffin pan onto the center of the rack, and close the door.
5. Serve and enjoy.

Pancetta & Spinach Frittata

Prep time: 15 minutes | Cook time: 16 minutes | Serves 2

- 60g pancetta
- ½ of tomato, cubed
- 3 eggs
- salt and ground black pepper, as required
- 60g Parmesan cheese, grated

1. Heat a nonstick skillet over medium heat and cook the pancetta for about 5 minutes
2. Add the tomato and spinach cook for about 2-3 minutes
3. Remove from the heat and drain the grease from skillet.
4. Set aside to cool slightly.
5. Press "Start/Pause" button to start.
6. When the unit beeps to show that it is preheated, open the oven door.
7. Arrange the pan over the wire rack and insert in the oven.
8. When cooking time is completed, open the oven door and remove the baking dish.
9. Cut into equal-sized wedges and serve.

Sausage Bake Omelet

Prep time: 5 minutes | Cook time: 45 minutes |Serves 8

- 16 egg
- 450g ground sausage
- 354ml almond milk
- 118ml salsa
- 1g paprika
- 470g mozzarella cheese, shredded
- Pepper
- Salt

1. Place rack in the bottom position and close door. Select bake mode set the temperature to 176℃ and set the timer to 45 minutes. Press the setting dial to preheat.
2. Add sausage to a pan and cook until browned. Drain excess fat.
3. In a large bowl, whisk egg and milk, paprika, pepper, and salt.
4. Stir in cheese, cooked sausage, and salsa.
5. Pour omelet mixture into the greased baking dish.
6. Serve and enjoy.

Chapter 3

Snacks and Appetizer Recipes

Tofu Nuggets

Prep time: 5 minutes | Cook time: 30 minutes |Serves 4

- 450g firm tofu, cut into cubes
- 15g paprika
- 30g Italian seasoning
- 15g garlic powder
- 30g onion powder
- 59ml rice flour
- 59ml Nutritional yeast flakes
- 450g liquid aminos
- 30g salt

1. Add tofu and liquid aminos into the mixing bowl. Mix well and let it marinate for 20 minutes.
2. In a separate bowl, add remaining ingredients and mix well. Add tofu and coat well.
3. Spray sheet pan with cooking spray.
4. Arrange tofu cubes on a greased sheet pan.
5. Select bake mode then set the temperature to 204℃ and time for 30 minutes. Press start.
6. Once the oven is preheated then place the sheet pan into the oven.
7. Turn tofu pieces halfway through.
8. Serve and enjoy.

Baked Mozzarella Sticks

Prep time: 5 minutes | Cook time: 8 minutes |Serves 6

- 118g Italian Style bread crumbs
- 177ml panko break crumbs
- 60g parmesan cheese
- 1 tablespoon garlic powder
- 12 mozzarella cheese sticks
- Cooking spray

1. Make mozzarella sticks by freezing them for an hour or two. Take the mozzarella sticks out of the fridge and cut them in half so that each one is 2-3 inches long.
2. Combine the Panko, Italian Style bread crumbs, parmesan cheese, and garlic powder on a dish and stir well.
3. Whisk together the egg in a separate bowl.
4. Cover the mozzarella stick completely with egg with a fork, then dip and totally cover the mozzarella stick in the breadcrumb mixture.
5. On a nonstick pan, arrange mozzarella sticks in a single layer.
6. Select the timer for 10 minutes and the temperature for 182℃.
7. Remove and serve.

Red Pepper Feta Dip

Prep time: 5 minutes | Cook time: 20 minutes | Serves 12

- 12 oz jar roasted red peppers, drained & chopped
- 1/2 lemon juice
- 60g olive oil
- 8 oz feta cheese, crumbled
- 15g pepper
- 30g dried oregano
- 59ml fresh basil, chopped
- 2 garlic cloves, minced
- 8 oz cream cheese, softened

1. In a mixing bowl, add roasted peppers, feta cheese, pepper, oregano, basil, garlic, and cream cheese and mix until well combined.
2. Pour mixture into the greased baking dish.
3. Select bake mode then set the temperature to 204℃ and time for 20 minutes. Press start.
4. Once the oven is preheated then place the baking dish into the oven.
5. Drizzle with oil and lemon juice.
6. Serve and enjoy.

Onion Rings

Prep time: 15 minutes | Cook time: 15 minutes | Serves 4

- 118g all-purpose flour
- 1 teaspoon paprika
- 1 teaspoon salt, divided
- 118g buttermilk
- 1 egg
- 236g panko breadcrumbs
- 2 tablespoons olive oil
- 1 large yellow sweet onion, sliced ½-inch-thick rings

1. Mix flour with paprika and salt on a plate.
2. Coat the onion rings with the flour mixture.
3. Beat egg with buttermilk in a bowl. Dip all the onion rings with the egg mixture.
4. Spread the breadcrumbs in a bowl.
5. Coat the onion rings with breadcrumbs.
6. Press the TIME/SLICE button and change the value to 15 minutes, then press Start/Pause to begin cooking.
7. Serve warm.

Pumpkin Fries

Prep time: 15 minutes | Cook time: 12 minutes | Serves 6

- 118g plain Greek yogurt
- 2 tablespoons maple syrup
- 3 teaspoons chipotle peppers in adobo sauce, minced
- ⅛ teaspoon salt
- 1 medium pie pumpkin
- ¼ teaspoon pepper

1. Peel and cut the pumpkin into sticks.
2. Mix garlic powder, cumin, chili powder, salt, and black pepper.
3. Coat the pumpkin sticks with the spice mixture.
4. Spread the pumpkin fries in the air fry basket and spray them with cooking spray.
5. Serve fries with the sauce.

Easy Corn Dip

Prep time: 5 minutes | Cook time: 25 minutes | Serves 10

- 709g frozen corn kernels, thawed
- 15 oz sour cream
- 470g cheddar cheese, shredded
- 118ml bacon, cooked & chopped
- 1 oz ranch seasoning
- 8 oz cream cheese, softened

1. Add corn and remaining ingredients into the large bowl and mix until well combined.
2. Pour mixture into the baking dish.
3. Select bake mode then set the temperature to 204℃ and time for 25 minutes. Press start.
4. Once the oven is preheated then place the baking dish into the oven.
5. Serve and enjoy.

Beef Taquitos

Prep time: 15 minutes | Cook time: 8 minutes | Serves 6

- 6 corn tortillas
- 780g cooked beef, shredded
- 118g onion, chopped
- 236g pepper jack cheese, shredded
- olive oil cooking spray

1. Arrange the tortillas onto a smooth surface.
2. Place the shredded meat over one corner of each tortilla, followed by onion and cheese.
3. Roll each tortilla to secure the filling and secure with toothpicks.
4. Spray each taquito with cooking spray evenly.
5. Arrange the taquitos onto the greased sheet pan.
6. When cooking time is completed, open the oven door and transfer the taquitos onto a platter.
7. Serve warm.

Cinnamon Sugar Pinwheels

Prep time: 5 minutes | Cook time: 10 minutes | Serves 16

- 1 (9-inch) store-bought refrigerated pie dough
- 42 grams unsalted butter, at room temperature
- 50 grams packed light brown sugar
- 4 grams ground cinnamon
- 1 gram kosher salt
- Cooking spray

1. Unfold the pie dough and place it on a clean (unfloured) work surface.
2. In a medium bowl, stir together the butter, brown sugar, cinnamon, and salt until smooth. Use an offset spatula or butter knife to smear this mixture in a thin layer over the entire surface of the pie dough.
3. Roll the pie dough into a log as tightly as possible, being careful not to tear it. Using a sharp knife, cut the log crosswise into 1.3 cm-wide pieces, discarding the ends of the log.

Cheesy Broccoli Bites

Prep time: 15 minutes | Cook time: 12 minutes | Serves 5

- 236g broccoli florets
- 1 egg, beaten
- 180g cheddar cheese, grated
- 2 tablespoons Parmesan cheese, grated
- 180g panko breadcrumbs
- salt and freshly ground black pepper, as needed

1. In a food processor, add the broccoli and pulse until finely crumbled.
2. In a large bowl, mix together the broccoli and remaining ingredients.
3. Make small equal-sized balls from the mixture.
4. Press "Power" button of Ninja Foodi Digital Air Fry Oven and turn the dial to select "Air Fry" mode.
5. Press TIME/SLICE button and again turn the dial to set the cooking time to 12 minutes
6. Press "Start/Pause" button to start.
7. Serve warm.

Air Fryer Ravioli

Prep time: 5 minutes | Cook time: 10 minutes |Serves 2

- 12 frozen ravioli
- 118g buttermilk
- 118g Italian breadcrumbs
- Cooking oil

1. Place two bowls next to each other. In one, put the buttermilk, and in the other, put the breadcrumbs.
2. Dip Each ravioli piece in buttermilk and then breadcrumbs, making sure it is well coated.
3. Place each breaded ravioli in a single layer in the air fry basket and spritz the tops halfway through with oil.
4. Place it inside the oven.
5. Turn on Ninja Foodi Dual Heat Air Fry Oven and rotate the knob to select "Air Fry".
6. Select the timer for 7 minutes and the temperature for 200℃.
7. Remove from Ninja Foodi Dual Heat Air Fry Oven to serve hot.

Papas Bravas

Prep time: 15 minutes | Cook time: 35 minutes | Serves 4

- 28 grams unsalted butter
- 10 grams sweet paprika
- 5 grams hot smoked paprika
- 355 ml canned tomato sauce
- 15 grams minced fresh oregano
- 15 grams sugar
- 15 ml hot sauce of choice
- 2.5 grams onion powder
- 1.25 grams garlic powder
- 5 grams kosher salt
- 680 grams baby yellow potatoes
- 30 ml peanut oil or vegetable oil

1. Add the butter and both paprikas to the Foodi's inner pot and set the Foodi to Sear/Saute on High. Stir until the butter is bubbling, about 3 minutes.
2. Add the potatoes to the inner pot along with the oil and the remaining 1/2 teaspoon salt. Stir to coat the potatoes with the oil and then transfer them to the Crisping Basket. Set the basket into the inner pot, drop the Crisping Lid, and set the Foodi to Air Crisp at 200°C for 25 minutes, or until the potatoes are crisp and browned. Serve hot with the sauce.

Cherry Clafoutis

Prep time: 15 minutes | Cook time: 30 minutes | Serves 4

- 28 grams unsalted butter, melted, plus some at room temperature for greasing the pan
- 240 ml whole milk
- 3 large eggs
- 70 grams granulated sugar
- 5 ml vanilla extract
- 60 grams all-purpose flour
- 140 grams pitted and halved cherries, thawed if previously frozen
- Confectioners' sugar

1. Grease the bottom and sides of a 23 cm springform pan with a little butter and set aside (if the springform is not watertight, line it with foil to prevent leakage).
2. In a medium bowl, whisk together the milk, eggs, granulated sugar, vanilla, and 28 grams melted butter, whisking until the sugar is dissolved. Add the flour and whisk to combine.
3. Release the latch from the springform pan and remove the ring. Transfer the clafoutis (still on the pan base) to a large plate. Dust with confectioners' sugar (you can sift the sugar through a fine sieve or use a shaker) and serve warm.

Chapter 4

Beef, Pork and Lamb Recipes

Garlic Balsamic Lamb Chops

Prep time: 5 minutes | Cook time: 15 minutes |Serves 4

- 4 lamb chops
- 30g garlic, crushed
- 60g canola oil
- 59ml balsamic vinegar
- 15g onion powder
- 15g paprika
- Pepper
- Salt

1. Select air fry mode set the temperature to 204℃ and set the timer to 15 minutes. Press the setting dial to preheat.
2. Add lamb chops and remaining ingredients into the zip-lock bag. Seal bag and place in refrigerator for 60 minutes.
3. Place lamb chops into the air fryer basket.
4. Once the unit is preheated, open the door, and place the air fryer basket on the top level of the oven, and close the door.
5. Serve and enjoy.

Garlicky Lamb Chops

Prep time: 15 minutes | Cook time: 45 minutes | Serves 8

- 8 medium lamb chops
- 60g olive oil
- 3 thin lemon slices
- 2 garlic cloves, crushed
- 1 teaspoon dried oregano
- 1 teaspoon salt
- ½ teaspoon black pepper

1. Place the medium lamb chops in a sheet pan and rub them with olive oil.
2. Add lemon slices, garlic, oregano, salt, and black pepper on top of the lamb chops.
3. Transfer the tray to the Ninja Foodi Digital Air Fry Oven and close the door.
4. Select "Air Roast" mode by rotating the dial.
5. Press the TIME/SLICE button and change the value to 45 minutes
6. Press the TEMP/DARKNESS button and change the value to 200℃.
7. Press Start/Pause to begin cooking.
8. Serve warm.

Rump Steak

Prep time: 5 minutes | Cook time: 15 minutes |Serves: 2

- 2 pounds of rump steak
- 2onions, sliced
- 1 green bell pepper, sliced
- Salt and black pepper, to taste
- 118g parmesan cheese
- 4 Hoagies roll, as needed

1. Take a Ninja Foodi Digital Air Fry Oven and grease it with a mesh tray.
2. Place the steak, bell pepper, and onion in a bowl and season it with salt and black pepper. Then place it on a baking tray.
3. Preheat the Ninja Foodi Digital Air Fry Oven for 198℃ for 5 minutes.
4. Put the tray in the Oven and bake for 10 minutes at 176℃.
5. Once done, place it on a hoagie roll and layer the shredded parmesan on top.
6. Serve and enjoy.

Flavorful Pork Patties

Prep time: 5 minutes | Cook time: 10 minutes |Serves: 2

- 226g ground pork
- 1 egg, lightly beaten
- 118ml breadcrumbs
- 1g paprika
- 1/8 tsp cayenne
- 15g Italian seasoning
- Pepper
- Salt

1. Add all ingredients into the large bowl and mix until well combined.
2. Make patties from the meat mixture and place them in an air fryer basket.
3. Select air fry then set the temperature to 182℃ and time for 10 minutes. Press start.
4. Once the oven is preheated then place the basket into the top rails of the oven.
5. Turn patties halfway through.
6. Serve and enjoy.

Meatloaf

Prep time: 5 minutes | Cook time: 60 minutes | Serves 8

- 3 egg
- 4 oz sharp cheddar cheese, shredded
- 59ml green pepper, diced
- 118ml onion, chopped
- 1g black pepper
- 45 crackers, crushed
- 1 226g lean ground beef
- 118ml milk
- 30g salt

1. In a mixing bowl, beat the egg then add cheese, green pepper, onion, cracker crumbs, milk pepper, and salt. Stir well to combine.
2. Add ground meat and mix well.
3. Make a loaf of meat mixture and place on a sheet pan.
4. Select bake mode then set the temperature to 176℃ and time for 60 minutes. Press start.
5. Once the oven is preheated then place the sheet pan into the oven.
6. Serve and enjoy.

Greek lamb Farfalle

Prep time: 15 minutes | Cook time: 20 minutes | Serves 6

- 1 tablespoon olive oil
- 1 onion, chopped
- 2 garlic cloves, chopped
- 2 teaspoons dried oregano
- 450g pack lamb mince
- 337g tin tomatoes, chopped
- 60g black olives pitted
- 118g frozen spinach, defrosted
- 2 tablespoons dill, removed and chopped
- 250g farfalle paste, boiled
- 1 ball half-fat mozzarella, torn

1. Sauté onion and garlic with oil in a pan over moderate heat for 5 minutes
2. Stir in tomatoes, spinach, dill, oregano, lamb, and olives, then stir cook for 5 minutes
3. Spread the lamb in a casserole dish and toss in the boiled Farfalle pasta.
4. Top the pasta lamb mix with mozzarella cheese.
5. Press Start/Pause to begin cooking.
6. Serve warm.

Lamb and Vegetable Curry

Prep time: 15 Minutes | Cook time: 1 Hour | Serves 4

- 500 grams lamb shoulder, diced
- 2 tablespoons vegetable oil
- 1 large onion, finely chopped
- 3 cloves garlic, minced
- 1 tablespoon ginger, grated
- 2 tablespoons curry powder
- 1 teaspoon ground cumin
- 1 teaspoon ground coriander
- Salt and pepper to taste
- Fresh coriander, chopped (for garnish)
- Cooked rice (for serving)

1. In a large pot, heat the vegetable oil over medium heat. Add the diced lamb and brown on all sides. Remove the lamb from the pot and set aside.
2. In the same pot, add the chopped onion and cook until softened. Add the minced garlic and grated ginger, cooking for an additional 2 minutes.
3. Cover the pot and simmer for 45 minutes to 1 hour, or until the lamb is tender and the flavors have melded.
4. Garnish the Lamb and Vegetable Curry with chopped fresh coriander and serve over cooked rice.

Mustard Roasted Pork Tenderloin

Prep time: 15 minutes | Cook time: 25 minutes | Serves 4

- 1 large egg, lightly beaten
- 120 ml mayonnaise
- 60 ml grainy mustard
- 1/2 teaspoon freshly ground black pepper
- 60 grams all-purpose flour
- 1 teaspoon kosher salt
- 2 (450 grams each) pork tenderloins, patted dry and cut crosswise into thirds
- Cooking spray

1. In a shallow dish, whisk together the egg, mayonnaise, mustard, and pepper. Combine the flour and salt in another shallow dish.
2. Drop the Crisping Lid and set the Foodi to Bake/Roast at 190°C for 15 minutes, or until the crust on the tenderloin is set and an instant-read thermometer inserted into a piece of meat reads 63°C.
3. Lift the lid and let the tenderloin pieces rest in the Foodi for 5 minutes. Transfer the meat to a cutting board, slice it crosswise into round pieces, and serve warm.

Shepherd's Pie

Prep time: 20 Minutes | Cook time: 40 Minutes | Serves 4

- 500 grams ground lamb
- 1 tablespoon vegetable oil
- 1 onion, finely chopped
- 2 carrots, diced
- 2 cloves garlic, minced
- 2 tablespoons tomato paste
- 300 ml beef or lamb stock
- 50 grams unsalted butter
- 100 ml milk
- Salt and pepper to taste
- Chopped fresh parsley (for garnish)

1. Preheat the oven to 200°C (180°C fan).
2. In a large pan, heat the vegetable oil over medium heat. Add the ground lamb and cook until browned. Remove any excess fat.
3. Add the chopped onion, diced carrots, and minced garlic to the pan. Cook until the vegetables are softened.
4. Stir in the tomato paste and cook for 2 minutes. Sprinkle the flour over the mixture and stir to combine.
5. Garnish with chopped fresh parsley before serving.

Italian Sausages with Polenta and Grapes

Prep time: 10 Minutes | Cook time: 20 Minutes | Serves 6

- 900 grams seedless red grapes
- 3 shallots, sliced
- 2 teaspoons fresh thyme or 1 teaspoon dried thyme
- 30 ml extra-virgin olive oil
- 2.5 grams kosher salt or 1.25 grams fine salt
- Freshly ground black pepper
- 6 links (about 680 grams) hot or sweet Italian sausage
- 45 ml sherry vinegar or balsamic vinegar
- 6 (2.5 cm-thick) slices Oven Polenta or store-bought variety

1. Place the grapes in a large bowl. Add the shallots, thyme, olive oil, salt, and pepper. Gently toss. Place the grapes on the sheet pan. Arrange the sausage links evenly on the pan.
2. Select AIR ROAST, set the temperature to 190°C, and set the time to 20 minutes. Select START/PAUSE to begin preheating.
3. When cooking is complete, the grapes should be very soft, and the sausages browned.

Beef Short Ribs

Prep time: 5 minutes | Cook time: 8 minutes | Serves: 4

- 2pounds bone-in beef short ribs
- 3 tablespoons scallions, chopped
- ½ tablespoon fresh ginger, finely grated
- 118g low-sodium soy sauce
- 60g balsamic vinegar
- ½ tablespoon Sriracha
- 1 tablespoon sugar
- ½ teaspoon ground black pepper

1. In a resalable bag, place all the ingredients. Seal the bag and shake to coat well. Refrigerate overnight.
2. Select the "AIR CRISP" function on your Ninja Foodi Digital Air Fry Oven.
3. Press "Temp Button" and use the dial to set the temperature at 196℃.
4. Now press the "Time Button" and use the dial to set the cooking time to 8 minutes.
5. Press the "START/PAUSE" button to start.
6. Place the ribs into the greased Air Crisp Basket and insert them in the oven.
7. Flip the ribs once halfway through.
8. When the cooking time is completed, open the door and serve hot.

Ravioli with Meat Sauce

Prep time: 10 Minutes | Cook time: 10 Minutes | Serves 4

- 1 (567-gram) package frozen cheese ravioli
- 1 teaspoon kosher salt or 1/2 teaspoon fine salt
- 295 ml water
- 6 Scratch Meatballs, crumbled
- 600 ml Marinara Sauce or store-bought variety
- 30 grams grated Parmesan cheese, for garnish

1. Place the ravioli in an even layer on the sheet pan. Stir the salt into the water until dissolved and pour it over the ravioli.
2. Select BAKE, set temperature to 230°C, and set time to 10 minutes. Select START/PAUSE to begin preheating.
3. Once the unit has preheated, slide the pan into the oven.
4. When cooking is complete, remove the pan from the oven. The ravioli should be tender, and the sauce heated through. Gently stir the ingredients. Serve the ravioli with the Parmesan cheese, if desired.

Greek Pork Chops

Prep time: 5 minutes | **Cook time:** 25 minutes | **Serves:** 6

- 6 pork chops
- 118ml basil pesto
- 60g olive oil
- Pepper
- Salt

1. Brush pork chops with oil and season with pepper and salt.
2. Place pork chops into the baking dish.
3. Pour pesto over pork chops.
4. Select bake mode then set the temperature to 218℃ and time for 25 minutes. Press start.
5. Once the oven is preheated then place the baking dish into the oven.
6. Serve and enjoy.

Glazed Beef Short Ribs

Prep time: 15 minutes | **Cook time:** 8 minutes | **Serves 4**

- 900g bone-in beef short ribs
- 3 tablespoons scallions, chopped
- ½ tablespoon fresh ginger, finely grated
- 118g low-sodium soy sauce
- 60g balsamic vinegar
- ½ tablespoon Sriracha
- 1 tablespoon sugar
- ½ teaspoon ground black pepper

1. In a resealable bag, place all the ingredients.
2. Seal the bag and shake to coat well.
3. Refrigerate overnight.
4. Flip the ribs once halfway through.
5. When the cooking time is completed, open the oven door and serve hot.

Pork Fried Rice with Mushrooms and Peas

Prep time: 10 Minutes | Cook time: 12 Minutes | Serves 4

- 120 grams 3 spring onions, diced
- 1/2 red bell pepper, diced (about 120 grams)
- 10 ml sesame oil
- 240 ml Oven-Roasted Mushrooms
- 480 ml Oven Rice
- 1 egg, beaten

1. Place the spring onions and red pepper on the sheet pan. Drizzle with the sesame oil and toss the vegetables to coat them in the oil.
2. Select AIR ROAST, set the temperature to 190°C, and set the time to 12 minutes. Select START/PAUSE to begin preheating.
3. When cooking is complete, remove the pan from the oven and stir the egg to scramble it. Stir the egg into the fried rice mixture. Serve immediately.

Beef Patties

Prep time: 5 minutes | Cook time: 25 minutes | Serves: 6

- 2 egg, lightly beaten
- 450g ground beef
- 15g chili powder
- 236ml breadcrumbs
- 1/2 onion, chopped
- 2 courgette, grated and squeezed
- Pepper
- Salt

1. Add all ingredients into the large bowl and mix until well combined.
2. Make small patties from the meat mixture and place them on a sheet pan.
3. Select bake mode then set the temperature to 204℃ and time for 25 minutes. Press start.
4. Once the oven is preheated then place the sheet pan into the oven.
5. Serve and enjoy.

Chapter 5

Poultry Recipes

Thanksgiving Turkey

Prep time: 5 minutes | Cook time: 35 minutes | Serves: 4

- 1 turkey breast
- Kosher salt and black pepper, to taste
- 1 teaspoon thyme, chopped
- 1 teaspoon rosemary, chopped
- 1 teaspoon sage, chopped
- 60g maple syrup
- 2 tablespoons Dijon mustard
- 1 tablespoon. butter, melted

1. Rub the turkey breast with maple syrup, Dijon mustard, butter, black pepper, and herbs.
2. Place the turkey in a baking tray and set it in the Ninja Foodi Digital Air Fry Oven.
3. Select the "AIR CRISP" mode using the function keys.
4. Set its cooking time to 35 minutes and temperature to 198℃
5. Press "START/PAUSE" to initiate preheating.
6. Serve warm.

Tasty Chicken Drumsticks

Prep time: 5 minutes | Cook time: 20 minutes | Serves: 4

- 4 chicken drumsticks
- 177g teriyaki sauce
- 1.8kg green onion, chopped
- 450g sesame seeds, toasted

1. Select air fry mode set the temperature to 182℃ and set the timer to 20 minutes. Press the setting dial to preheat.
2. Add chicken drumsticks and teriyaki sauce into the zip-lock bag. Seal bag and place in refrigerator for 1 hour.
3. Arrange marinated chicken drumsticks in the air fryer basket.
4. Once the unit is preheated, open the door, and place the air fryer basket on the top level of the oven, and close the door.
5. Garnish with green onion and sprinkle with sesame seeds.
6. Serve and enjoy.

Chicken Tomato Mushrooms Bake

Prep time: 5 minutes | Cook time: 30 minutes |Serves: 4

- 907g chicken breasts, halved
- 79ml sun-dried tomatoes
- 8 oz mushrooms, sliced
- 118ml mayonnaise
- 30g salt

1. Place rack in the bottom position and close door. Select bake mode set the temperature to 198℃ and set the timer to 30 minutes. Press the setting dial to preheat.
2. Place chicken into the baking dish and top with mushrooms, sun-dried tomatoes, mayonnaise, and salt. Mix well.
3. Once the unit is preheated, open the door, and place the baking dish onto the center of the rack, and close the door.
4. Serve and enjoy.

Chicken Casserole

Prep time: 5 minutes | Cook time: 25 minutes |Serves: 5

- 560g chicken, cooked and shredded
- 118ml water
- 8 oz cream cheese
- 5 oz green beans, chopped
- 59ml mozzarella cheese, shredded
- 59ml parmesan cheese, grated
- 15g garlic powder
- Salt

1. In a medium saucepan, heat heavy cream, parmesan cheese, garlic powder, cream cheese, water, and salt over low heat until smooth.
2. Add green beans into the greased baking dish.
3. Spread chicken on top of green beans.
4. Pour cream mixture over chicken and top with mozzarella.
5. Once the oven is preheated then place the baking dish into the oven.
6. Serve and enjoy.

Parmesan Chicken Tenders

Prep time: 15 minutes | Cook time: 15 minutes | Serves 4

- 118g flour
- salt and ground black pepper, as required
- 2 eggs, beaten
- 180g panko breadcrumbs
- 180g Parmesan cheese, grated finely
- 1 teaspoon Italian seasoning
- 8 chicken tenders

1. In a shallow dish, mix together the flour, salt and black pepper.
2. In a third shallow dish, mix together the breadcrumbs, parmesan cheese and Italian seasoning.
3. Coat the chicken tenders with flour mixture, then dip into the beaten eggs and finally coat with breadcrumb mixture.
4. Press "Start/Pause" button to start.
5. When the unit beeps to show that it is preheated, open the oven door and insert the sheet pan in oven.
6. When the cooking time is completed, open the oven door and serve hot.

Spicy Meatballs

Prep time: 5 minutes | Cook time: 20 minutes |Serves: 8

- 907g ground chicken
- 2 jalapeno chili pepper, chopped
- 8g ginger, grated
- 30g garlic, crushed
- 90g breadcrumbs
- 59ml fresh basil, chopped
- 59ml scallions, sliced
- 450g ground coriander
- 450g fish sauce
- Pepper
- Salt

1. Add all ingredients into the bowl and mix until well combined.
2. Make small balls from the mixture and place them on a sheet pan.
3. Select bake mode then set the temperature to 198℃ and time for 20 minutes. Press start.
4. Once the oven is preheated then place the sheet pan into the oven.
5. Serve and enjoy.

The Ultimate UK Ninja Foodi Dual Zone Air Fryer Cookbook

Chicken and Mushroom Pie

Prep time: 20 Minutes | Cook time: 40 Minutes | Serves 4

- 400 grams chicken breast, diced
- 1 tablespoon vegetable oil
- 1 onion, finely chopped
- 200 grams mushrooms, sliced
- 2 tablespoons all-purpose flour
- 300 ml chicken stock
- 150 ml whole milk
- Salt and pepper to taste
- 1 sheet ready-rolled puff pastry
- 1 egg, beaten (for egg wash)

1. Preheat the oven to 200°C (180°C fan).
2. In a large pan, heat the vegetable oil over medium heat. Add the diced chicken and cook until browned. Remove the chicken from the pan and set aside.
3. In the same pan, add the chopped onion and sliced mushrooms. Cook until the vegetables are softened.
4. Allow the pie to cool for a few minutes before serving.

Chicken Taquitos

Prep time: 5 minutes | Cook time: 20 minutes | Serves 6

- 225 grams shredded cooked chicken
- 150 grams shredded Mexican-style cheese
- 60 ml your favorite salsa
- 6 (8-inch) flour tortillas
- Cooking spray

1. Combine the chicken, cheese, and salsa in a medium bowl, mashing until it holds together.
2. Shape 60 ml of the chicken mixture into a log and place it in the center of a tortilla, then tightly roll it up, securing it with a toothpick. Repeat with the remaining filling and tortillas.
3. Drop the Crisping Lid and set to Air Crisp at 200°C for 15 minutes, or until the taquitos are golden and crisp, rotating the positioning of the taquitos every 5 minutes. Allow them to cool slightly before serving with salsa, sour cream, or nacho cheese for dipping.

Chicken Tikka Masala

Prep time: 15 Minutes | Cook time: 30 Minutes | Serves 4

- 500 grams chicken thighs, cut into bite-sized pieces
- 2 tablespoons vegetable oil
- 1 onion, finely chopped
- 2 cloves garlic, minced
- 1 tablespoon ginger, grated
- 1 teaspoon ground cumin
- 1 teaspoon ground coriander
- 1 teaspoon turmeric
- Fresh coriander, chopped (for garnish)
- Cooked rice (for serving)

1. In a large pan, heat the vegetable oil over medium heat. Add the chopped onion and cook until softened.
2. Add the minced garlic and grated ginger to the pan, stirring for 1-2 minutes until fragrant.
3. Add the chicken pieces to the pan and cook until browned on all sides.
4. Garnish the Chicken Tikka Masala with chopped fresh coriander and serve over cooked rice.

Parmesan Crusted Chicken Breasts

Prep time: 15 minutes | Cook time: 15 minutes | Serves 4

- 2 large chicken breasts
- 236g mayonnaise
- 236g Parmesan cheese, shredded
- 236g panko breadcrumbs

1. Cut each chicken breast in half and then with a meat mallet pound each into even thickness.
2. Spread the mayonnaise on both sides of each chicken piece evenly.
3. In a shallow bowl, mix together the Parmesan and breadcrumbs.
4. Coat the chicken piece Parmesan mixture evenly.
5. Press "Power" button of Ninja Foodi Digital Air Fry Oven and turn the dial to select "Air Fry" mode.
6. Press TIME/SLICE button and again turn the dial to set the cooking time to 15 minutes
7. When the cooking time is completed, open the oven door and serve hot.

Crispy Chicken Cutlets

Prep time: 15 minutes | Cook time: 30 minutes | Serves 4

- 180g flour
- 2 large eggs
- 1118gs breadcrumbs
- 60g Parmesan cheese, grated
- 1 tablespoon mustard powder
- salt and ground black pepper, as required
- 4 (6-ounce) (¼-inch thick) skinless, boneless chicken cutlets

1. In a shallow bowl, add the flour.
2. In a second bowl, crack the eggs and beat well.
3. In a third bowl, mix together the breadcrumbs, cheese, mustard powder, salt, and black pepper.
4. Season the chicken with salt, and black pepper.
5. When cooking time is completed, open the oven door and serve hot.

Balsamic Chicken

Prep time: 5 minutes | Cook time: 25 minutes |Serves: 4

- 4 chicken breasts, skinless and boneless
- 118ml balsamic vinegar
- 60g soy sauce
- 59ml olive oil
- 8g dried oregano
- 2 garlic cloves, minced
- Pepper
- Salt

1. Place rack in the bottom position and close door. Select bake mode set the temperature to 198℃ and set the timer to 25 minutes. Press the setting dial to preheat.
2. In a bowl, mix together soy sauce, oil, pepper, oregano, garlic, and vinegar.
3. Place chicken in a baking dish and pour soy sauce mixture over chicken.
4. Serve and enjoy.

Greek Chicken Casserole

Prep time: 5 minutes | Cook time: 25 minutes |Serves: 6

- 470g rotisserie chicken, shredded
- 8 corn tortillas
- 354ml salsa
- 236ml sour cream
- 470g Monterey jack cheese, shredded
- 470g tomatoes, chopped

1. In a bowl, mix together chicken, 236ml cheese, tomatoes, salsa, and sour cream.
2. Transfer chicken mixture into the greased baking dish.
3. Top with tortillas and remaining cheese.
4. Select bake mode then set the temperature to 204℃ and time for 25 minutes. Press start.
5. Once the oven is preheated then place the baking dish into the oven.
6. Serve and enjoy.

Cheesy Chicken

Prep time: 5 minutes | Cook time: 55 minutes |Serves: 4

- 4 chicken breasts
- 30g dried basil
- 30g dried oregano
- 236ml parmesan cheese, grated
- 236ml half and half
- 236ml cheddar cheese, shredded
- Pepper
- Salt

1. Place chicken breasts into the greased baking dish and top with cheddar cheese.
2. In a bowl, mix parmesan cheese, half and half, oregano, basil, pepper, and salt.
3. Pour cheese mixture over chicken breasts.
4. Once the oven is preheated then place the baking dish into the oven.
5. Serve and enjoy.

Chapter 6

Fish and Seafood Recipes

Cod Parcel

Prep time: 5 minutes | Cook time: 23 minutes |Serves: 4

- 2 cod fillets
- 6 asparagus stalks
- 60g white sauce
- 1 teaspoon oil
- 60g champagne
- Salt and ground black pepper, as required

1. In a bowl, mix together all the ingredients.
2. Divide the cod mixture over 2 pieces of foil evenly.
3. Seal the foil around the cod mixture to form the packet.
4. Press AIR OVEN MODE button of Ninja Foodi Dual Heat Air Fry Oven and turn the dial to select "Air Fry" mode.
5. Press "Start/Stop" button to start.
6. When the unit beeps to show that it is preheated, open the oven door.
7. Carefully the parcels and serve hot.

Tuna Patties

Prep time: 5 minutes | Cook time: 6 minutes |Serves: 4

- 1 egg, lightly beaten
- 8 oz can tuna, drained
- 1g garlic powder
- 59ml breadcrumbs
- 450g mustard
- Pepper
- Salt

1. Add all ingredients into the large bowl and mix until well combined.
2. Make patties from the mixture and place them in an air fryer basket.
3. Select air fry then set the temperature to 204℃ and time for 6 minutes. Press start.
4. Once the oven is preheated then place the basket into the top rails of the oven.
5. Turn patties halfway through.
6. Serve and enjoy.

Shrimp Scampi

Prep time: 5 minutes | Cook time: 10 minutes |Serves: 4

- 907g shrimp, peeled
- 118ml fresh lime juice
- 59ml butter, sliced
- 177g olive oil
- 8g dried oregano
- 450g garlic, minced
- Pepper
- Salt

1. Add shrimp to a baking dish.
2. In a bowl, whisk together lemon juice, oregano, garlic, oil, pepper, and salt and pour over shrimp.
3. Spread butter on top of shrimp.
4. Select bake mode then set the temperature to 176℃ and time for 10 minutes. Press start.
5. Serve and enjoy.

Greek Shrimp

Prep time: 5 minutes | Cook time: 25 minutes |Serves: 4

- 450g shrimp, peeled
- 450g garlic, sliced
- 470g cherry tomatoes
- 450g olive oil
- Pepper
- Salt

1. Add shrimp, oil, garlic, tomatoes, pepper, and salt into the bowl and toss well.
2. Transfer shrimp mixture into the baking dish.
3. Select bake mode then set the temperature to 204℃ and time for 25 minutes. Press start.
4. Once the oven is preheated then place the baking dish into the oven.
5. Serve and enjoy.

Honey Mustard Salmon with Asparagus

Prep time: 10 Minutes | Cook time: 15 Minutes | Serves 4

- 4 (170 grams each) salmon fillets, with or without skin
- 5 grams kosher salt or 2.5 grams fine salt, divided
- 15 ml honey
- 10 ml Dijon mustard
- 30 grams unsalted butter, melted, or extra-virgin olive oil for dairy-free
- 900 grams asparagus, trimmed
- Lemon wedges, for serving

1. Sprinkle the salmon on both sides with 2.5 grams of kosher salt.
2. In a small bowl, whisk together the honey, mustard, and 15 ml of butter.
3. Place the asparagus on the sheet pan. Drizzle with the remaining 15 ml of butter and sprinkle with the remaining 2.5 grams of salt. Toss to coat. Move the asparagus to the outside of the sheet pan.
4. When cooking is complete, remove the pan from the oven. Place the salmon and asparagus on a plate. Squeeze a little lemon juice over the fish and vegetables, and serve.

Basil Garlic Shrimp

Prep time: 5 minutes | Cook time: 10 minutes |Serves: 4

- 907g shrimp, shelled & deveined
- 450g fresh lemon juice
- 79ml dry white wine
- 8g garlic, minced
- 118ml basil, shredded
- 180g butter
- 60g sun-dried tomatoes, chopped
- 1 1/60g olive oil

1. Season shrimp with pepper and salt. Heat oil in a pan over high heat.
2. Add shrimp to the pan and sauté for 1 minute per side.
3. Transfer shrimp to the baking dish.
4. Select bake mode then set the temperature to 176℃ and time for 7 minutes. Press start.
5. Once the oven is preheated then place the baking dish into the oven.
6. Meanwhile, add garlic in the same pan and cook for 15 seconds, then stir in tomatoes, lemon juice, and wine, stir until liquid reduced by 2/3.
7. Add basil and butter and stir until butter is melted. Season with pepper and salt. Pour sauce over shrimp and serve.

Lobster Tail Casserole

Prep time: 5 minutes | Cook time: 16 minutes |Serves 6

- 1 pound salmon fillets, cut into 8 equal pieces
- 16 large sea scallops
- 16 large prawns, peeled and deveined
- 8 East Coast lobster tails split in half
- 78g butter
- 60g white wine
- 60g lemon juice
- 2 tablespoons chopped fresh tarragon
- 2 medium garlic cloves, minced
- ½ teaspoon paprika
- ¼ teaspoon ground cayenne pepper

1. Whisk butter with lemon juice, wine, garlic, tarragon, paprika, salt, and cayenne pepper in a small saucepan.
2. Stir cook this mixture over medium heat for 1 minute.
3. Toss scallops, salmon fillet, and prawns in the SearPlate and pour the butter mixture on top.
4. Transfer the dish to Ninja Foodi Dual Heat Air Fry Oven and close the door.
5. Select "Bake" mode by rotating the dial.
6. Press Start/Stop to begin cooking.
7. Serve warm.

Baked Tilapia with Buttery Crumb Topping

Prep time: 5 minutes | Cook time: 16 minutes |Serves 4

- 4 tilapia fillets
- Salt and black pepper to taste
- 236ml bread crumbs
- 3 tablespoons butter, melted
- ½ teaspoon dried basil

1. Rub the tilapia fillets with black pepper and salt, then place them in the SearPlate.
2. Mix butter, breadcrumbs, and seasoning in a bowl.
3. Sprinkle the breadcrumbs mixture on top of the tilapia.
4. Transfer the SearPlate to Ninja Foodi Dual Heat Air Fry Oven and close the door.
5. Select "Bake" mode by rotating the dial.
6. Press the TIME/SLICES button and change the value to 15 minutes.
7. Press the TEMP/SHADE button and change the value to 190℃.
8. Press Start/Stop to begin cooking.
9. Switch to "Broil" at "HI" and cook for 1 minute.
10. Serve warm.

Teriyaki Salmon with Baby Bok Choy

Prep time: 15 Minutes | Cook time: 15 Minutes | Serves 4

- 180 ml Teriyaki Sauce or store-bought variety
- 4 (170 grams each) skinless salmon fillets
- 4 heads baby bok choy, root ends trimmed off and cut in half lengthwise through the root
- 15 ml vegetable oil
- 15 ml toasted sesame seeds

1. Set aside 60 ml of Teriyaki Sauce and pour the rest into a resealable plastic bag. Place the salmon in the bag and seal, squeezing as much air out as possible. Let the salmon marinate for at least 10 minutes (longer if you have the time).
2. Place the bok choy halves on the sheet pan. Drizzle the vegetable and sesame oils over the vegetables and toss to coat. Drizzle about a tablespoon of the reserved Teriyaki Sauce over the bok choy, then push them to the sides of the pan.
3. When cooking is complete, remove the pan from the oven. Brush the salmon with the remaining Teriyaki Sauce. Garnish with the sesame seeds. Serve with steamed rice, if desired.

Salmon & Asparagus Parcel

Prep time: 15 minutes | Cook time: 13 minutes | Serves 2

- 2 (4-ounce) salmon fillets
- 6 asparagus stalks
- 60g white sauce
- 1 teaspoon oil
- 60g champagne
- salt and ground black pepper, as required

1. In a bowl, mix together all the ingredients.
2. Divide the salmon mixture over 2 pieces of foil evenly.
3. Seal the foil around the salmon mixture to form the packet.
4. Press "Power" button of Ninja Foodi Digital Air Fry Oven and turn the dial to select "Air Fry" mode.
5. Press TIME/SLICE button and again turn the dial to set the cooking time to 13 minutes
6. Press "Start/Pause" button to start.
7. When the unit beeps to show that it is preheated, open the oven door.
8. Arrange the salmon parcels into the air fry basket and insert in the oven.
9. When cooking time is completed, open the oven door and serve hot.

Seafood Casserole

Prep time: 15 minutes | Cook time: 20 minutes | Serves 8

- 227g haddock, skinned and diced
- 450g scallops
- 450g large shrimp, peeled and deveined
- 3 to 4 garlic cloves, minced
- 118g heavy cream
- 118g Swiss cheese, shredded
- 2 tablespoons Parmesan, grated
- paprika, to taste
- Sea salt and black pepper, to taste

1. Toss shrimp, scallops, and haddock chunks in the sheet pan greased with cooking spray.
2. Drizzle salt, black pepper, and minced garlic over the seafood mix.
3. Top this seafood with cream, Swiss cheese, paprika, and Parmesan cheese.
4. Press the TIME/SLICE button and change the value to 20 minutes
5. Press Start/Pause to begin cooking.
6. Serve warm.

Salmon Patties

Prep time: 5 minutes | Cook time: 20 minutes | Serves: 4

- 2 egg, lightly beaten
- 59ml breadcrumbs
- 118ml fresh parsley, chopped
- 30g Dijon mustard
- 14 oz can salmon, drained and flaked
- 450g garlic, minced
- 1g pepper
- 15g kosher salt

1. Add all ingredients into the bowl and mix until well combined.
2. Spray sheet pan with cooking spray.
3. Make patties from the mixture and place them on a greased sheet pan.
4. Select bake mode then set the temperature to 204℃ and time for 20 minutes. Press start.
5. Once the oven is preheated then place the sheet pan into the oven.
6. Turn patties halfway through.
7. Serve and enjoy.

Chapter 7

Vegetables and Sides Recipes

Potato Croquettes

Prep time: 5 minutes | Cook time: 1 Hour | Serves 6

- 470g sweet potatoes, mashed
- 470g quinoa, cooked
- 60g celery, diced
- 60g scallions, chopped
- 60g parsley, chopped
- 60g flour
- 2 teaspoon Italian seasoning
- 2 garlic cloves, minced
- Salt and pepper to taste

1. Spray sheet pan with cooking spray and set aside.
2. Add all ingredients into the large bowl and mix well. Make 1-inch round croquettes from the mixture and place them on a sheet pan.
3. Place the wire rack inside your Ninja Foodi Digital Air Fry Oven.
4. Select "BAKE" mode set the temperature to 190℃, and set time to 60 minutes
5. Press "START/PAUSE" to begin preheating.
6. Cook for an hour.
7. Serve and enjoy.

Succotash

Prep time: 5 minutes | Cook time: 10 minutes | Serves 5

- Cooking oil spray
- 2.3kg fresh corn kernels
- 2 118g cherry tomatoes, halved
- 8 garlic cloves, minced
- 2 small onions, chopped
- 470g frozen lima beans
- 8 tablespoons unsalted butter, cut into small cubes
- Kosher salt and black pepper, to taste
- Thinly sliced fresh basil for garnish

1. Lightly coat the sheet pans with cooking spray.
2. Divide the corn, cherry tomatoes, garlic, onions, lima beans, and butter cubes between the two pans. Season with salt and pepper and thoroughly mix to combine.
3. Install the wire racks inside your Ninja Foodi Digital Air Fry Oven.
4. When the unit has preheated, place a sheet pan on each wire rack. Close the oven door to begin cooking.
5. After 10 minutes, open the oven and stir the vegetables. Close the oven door to continue cooking.

Stuffed Peppers

Prep time: 5 minutes | Cook time: 15 minutes | Serves 6

- 6 green bell peppers
- 1 pound lean ground beef
- 1 tablespoon olive oil
- 60g green onion, diced
- 60g fresh parsley
- ½ teaspoon ground sage
- ½ teaspoon garlic salt
- 236ml rice, cooked
- 236ml marinara sauce to taste
- 60g mozzarella cheese, shredded

1. Cook the ground beef in a medium sized skillet until it is well done.
2. Return the beef to the pan after draining it.
3. Combine the olive oil, green onion, parsley, sage, and salt in a large mixing bowl and add to the skillet with beef.
4. Add the cooked rice and marinara sauce in the skillet and stir this rice-beef mixture thoroughly.
5. Dish out to serve and enjoy.

Potato Casserole

Prep time: 5 minutes | Cook time: 50 minutes | Serves 6

- 2 egg
- 236ml cheddar cheese, shredded
- 10 potatoes, peeled, halved & boiled
- 90g butter
- 236ml sour cream
- 8 oz cream cheese, softened
- Pepper
- Salt

1. Mash the potatoes using masher until smooth.
2. Add remaining ingredients into the mashed potatoes and stir well to combine.
3. Pour potato mixture into the greased baking dish.
4. Select bake mode then set the temperature to 162℃ and time for 50 minutes. Press start.
5. Once the oven is preheated then place the baking dish into the oven.
6. Serve and enjoy.

Green Tomatoes

Prep time: 5 minutes | Cook time: 7 minutes |Serves 4

- 3 green tomatoes
- ½ teaspoon salt
- 118g flour
- 2 egg
- 79ml cornmeal
- 79ml breadcrumbs
- 1/8 teaspoon paprika

1. Slice the green tomatoes into ¼-inch slices and generously coat with salt. Allow for at least 5 minutes of resting time.
2. Put the flour in one bowl, the egg (whisked) in the second, and the cornmeal, breadcrumbs, and paprika in the third bowl to make a breading station.
3. Using a paper towel, pat green tomato slices dry.
4. Cook for 7-9 minutes, flipping and spritzing with oil halfway through.

Vegetable Nachos

Prep time: 5 minutes | Cook time: 5 minutes |Serves 3

- 8 ounces Tortilla chips
- 118g Grilled chicken
- 1 can Black beans, drained, rinsed
- 236ml White queso
- 118g Grape tomatoes, halved
- 78g Green onion, diced

1. Use foil to line the air fry basket.
2. Using a nonstick spray, coat the surface.
3. Assemble the nachos by layering the chips, chicken, and beans on top.
4. Place a layer of queso on top.
5. Add tomatoes and onions to the top.
6. Turn on Ninja Foodi Dual Heat Air Fry Oven and rotate the knob to select "Air Fry".
7. Select the timer for 5 minutes and the temperature for 180℃.
8. Remove from Ninja Foodi Dual Heat Air Fry Oven to serve.

Black Bean Veggie Burgers

Prep time: 15 minutes | Cook time: 20 minutes | Serves 4

- 400 grams Refried Black Beans (homemade or store-bought)
- 100 grams panko breadcrumbs
- 30 grams vegetable shortening
- 5 ml soy sauce
- 5 ml vegetarian Worcestershire sauce
- 3 drops liquid smoke
- 1/4 teaspoon dry mustard
- Cooking spray
- 4 burger buns

1. Place the refried beans, panko, shortening, soy sauce, Worcestershire, (If you plan to freeze the burgers for more than a day, wrap each in plastic wrap, then transfer the frozen burgers to a resealable plastic bag for up to a week.)
2. When ready to cook, set the Foodi to Sear/Saute on High and preheat for 5 minutes.
3. Serve the burgers on buns with the toppings of your choice.

Roast Cauliflower and Broccoli

Prep time: 5 minutes | Cook time: 10 minutes |Serves 4

- 226g broccoli, florets
- 226g cauliflower, florets
- 1 tablespoon olive oil
- Black pepper, to taste
- Salt, to taste
- 78g water

1. Toss all the veggies with seasoning in a large bowl.
2. Spread these vegetables in the air fry basket.
3. Transfer the basket to Ninja Foodi Dual Heat Air Fry Oven and close the door.
4. Select "Air Fry" mode by rotating the dial.
5. Press the TIME/SLICES button and change the value to 10 minutes.
6. Press the TEMP/SHADE button and change the value to 200℃.
7. Press Start/Stop to begin cooking.
8. Serve warm.

Japanese Curry

Prep time: 5 minutes | Cook time: 10 minutes | Serves 8

- 4 medium carrots, chopped
- 4 medium parsnips, chopped
- 454 grams fresh button mushrooms, sliced
- 2 medium russet potatoes, peeled and chopped
- 1/2 medium yellow onion, chopped
- 240 grams (1 package) hot Japanese curry bricks
- Steamed rice (optional)

1. Place the carrots, parsnips, mushrooms, potatoes, onion, and 1.4 liters water into the Foodi's inner pot. Lock on the Pressure Lid, making sure the valve is set to Seal, and set the Foodi to Pressure on High for 3 minutes. When the timer reaches 0, quick-release the pressure and carefully remove the lid.
2. Set the Foodi to Sear/Saute on High. Add the curry bricks and cook, stirring constantly, until the mixture is bubbling, about 3 minutes. Serve with white rice or on its own.

Caramelized Baby Carrots

Prep time: 10 minutes | Cook time: 15 minutes | Serves 4

- 118g butter, melted
- 118g brown sugar
- 450g bag baby carrots

1. In a bowl, mix together the butter, brown sugar and carrots.
2. Press "Power" button of Ninja Foodi Digital Air Fry Oven and turn the dial to select "Air Fry" mode.
3. Press TIME/SLICE button and again turn the dial to set the cooking time to 15 minutes
4. Now push TEMP/DARKNESS button and rotate the dial to set the temperature at 200℃.
5. Press "Start/Pause" button to start.
6. When the unit beeps to show that it is preheated, open the oven door.
7. Arrange the carrots in a greased air fry basket and insert in the oven.
8. When cooking time is completed, open the oven door and serve warm.

Quinoa Burgers

Prep time: 10 minutes | Cook time: 10 minutes | Serves 4

- 118g cooked and cooled quinoa
- 236g rolled oats
- 2 eggs, lightly beaten
- 60g white onion, minced
- 60g feta cheese, crumbled
- salt and ground black pepper, as required
- olive oil cooking spray

1. In a large bowl, add all ingredients and mix until well combined.
2. Make 4 equal-sized patties from the mixture.
3. Lightly spray the patties with cooking spray.
4. Press "Power" button of Ninja Foodi Digital Air Fry Oven and turn the dial to select "Air Fry" mode.
5. Press TIME/SLICE button and again turn the dial to set the cooking time to 10 minutes
6. Now push TEMP/DARKNESS button and rotate the dial to set the temperature at 200℃.
7. Press "Start/Pause" button to start.
8. Serve warm.

Orange and Saffron-Scented Rice Pilaf

Prep time: 15 minutes | Cook time: 35 minutes | Serves 4

- 45 ml peanut oil or vegetable oil
- 1/2 medium yellow onion, diced
- 1 garlic clove, minced
- Pinch of saffron threads
- 1/2 teaspoon dried orange peel
- 400 grams basmati rice
- 473 ml Foodi Chicken Stock (homemade or store-bought)
- 1 (283 grams) package frozen mixed vegetables
- 1/2 teaspoon kosher salt

1. Add the oil to the Foodi's inner pot and set the Foodi to Sear/Saute on High, heating for 5 minutes. Add the onion, garlic, saffron, and orange peel to the pot and cook until aromatic, about 4 minutes, stirring frequently.
2. Add the mixed vegetables. Drop the Crisping Lid and set the Foodi to Air Crisp at 200°C for 8 minutes, or until the vegetables are warmed through. Lift the lid and stir in the salt. Serve sprinkled with the scallions, paprika, and parsley.

Ham Hock Braised Greens

Prep time: 5 minutes | Cook time: 15 minutes | Serves 6

- 28 grams unsalted butter
- 1 medium yellow onion, diced
- 2 garlic cloves, minced
- 1 smoked ham hock
- 473 ml Foodi Chicken Stock (this page) or store-bought
- 907 grams collard greens, tough stems and ribs removed, leaves thinly sliced
- Juice of 1 lemon
- 2 teaspoons kosher salt

1. Add the butter to the Foodi's inner pot and set the Foodi to Sear/Saute on High until melted, about 4 minutes. Add the onion and garlic and cook until beginning to soften, about 6 minutes more, stirring occasionally.
2. Use tongs to remove the ham hock and set it aside to cool slightly before cutting the meat into chunks (discard the bone). Stir the ham back into the greens, then stir in the lemon juice and salt and serve.

Beans & Veggie Burgers

Prep time: 15 minutes | Cook time: 22 minutes | Serves 4

- 236g cooked black beans
- 780g boiled potatoes, peeled, and mashed
- 236g fresh spinach, chopped
- 236g fresh mushrooms, chopped
- 2 teaspoons Chile lime seasoning
- olive oil cooking spray

1. In a large bowl, add the beans, potatoes, spinach, mushrooms, and seasoning and with your hands, mix until well combined.
2. Make 4 equal-sized patties from the mixture.
3. Press "Power" button of Ninja Foodi Digital Air Fry Oven and turn the dial to select "Air Fry" mode.
4. Press TIME/SLICE button and again turn the dial to set the cooking time to 22 minutes
5. Flip the patties once after 12 minutes
6. When cooking time is completed, open the oven door and remove the air fry basket from the oven.

Broccoli & Rice

Prep time: 5 minutes | Cook time: 20 minutes |Serves 8

- 16 oz frozen broccoli florets
- 354ml cooked brown rice
- 1 large onion, chopped
- 1.8kg parmesan cheese, grated
- 10.5 oz condensed cheddar cheese soup
- 79ml milk
- 450g butter

1. Melt butter in a pan over medium heat.
2. Add onion and cook until tender.
3. Add broccoli and cook until broccoli is tender.
4. Stir in rice, soup, and milk and cook until hot.
5. Stir in cheese and pour the mixture into the baking dish.
6. Select bake mode then set the temperature to 176℃ and time for 20 minutes. Press start.
7. Once the oven is preheated then place the baking dish into the oven.
8. Serve and enjoy.

Cumin and Orange-Maple-Glazed Carrots

Prep time: 5 minutes | Cook time: 30 minutes | Serves 6

- 28 grams unsalted butter
- 5 grams ground cumin
- 907 grams carrots, cut into 2-inch pieces
- 120 ml orange juice
- 60 ml maple syrup
- 5 grams kosher salt

1. Place the butter and cumin in the Foodi's inner pot and set the Foodi to Sear/Saute until the butter is bubbling and aromatic, about 6 minutes.
2. Add the carrots and orange juice, then lock on the Pressure Lid, making sure the valve is set to Seal, and set to the timer reaches 0, quick-release the pressure and carefully remove the lid.
3. Stir in the maple syrup and salt. Set the Foodi to Air Crisp at 200°C for 20 minutes, or until the carrots are nicely browned. Serve warm or at room temperature if you want them to be a little stickier.

Chapter 8

Dessert Recipes

Cinnamon Rolls

Prep time: 5 minutes | Cook time: 30 minutes |Serves 6

- 2 tablespoons butter, melted
- 79ml packed brown sugar
- ½ teaspoon ground cinnamon
- Salt, to taste
- All-purpose flour for surface
- 56g cream cheese, softened
- 118g powdered sugar
- 1 tablespoon whole milk

1. Combine butter, brown sugar, cinnamon, and a large pinch of salt in a medium mixing bowl until smooth and fluffy.
2. Select the timer for 15 minutes and the temperature for LO.
3. Allow cooling for two minutes before serving.

Nutella Brownies

Prep time: 5 minutes | Cook time: 30 minutes |Serves 6

- 2 egg
- 118ml all-purpose flour
- 295ml Nutella
- 59ml cashews, chopped

1. In a bowl, mix together egg, flour, and Nutella until just combined.
2. Pour mixture into the greased baking pan and spread evenly. Sprinkle chopped cashews on top.
3. Select bake mode then set the temperature to 176℃ and time for 30 minutes. Press start.
4. Once the oven is preheated then place the baking dish into the oven.
5. Slice and serve.

Shortbread Fingers

Prep time: 15 minutes | Cook time: 12 minutes | Serves 10

- 80g caster sugar
- 390g plain flour
- 180g butter

1. In a large bowl, mix together the sugar and flour.
2. Add the butter and mix until a smooth dough forms.
3. Cut the dough into 10 equal-sized fingers.
4. with a fork, lightly prick the fingers.
5. Place the fingers into the lightly greased sheet pan.
6. Press "Power" button of Ninja Foodi Digital Air Fry Oven and turn the dial to select "Air Fry" mode.
7. Press TIME/SLICE button and again turn the dial to set the cooking time to 12 minutes
8. When cooking time is completed, open the oven door and place the baking pan onto a wire rack to cool for about 5-10 minutes
9. Now, invert the shortbread fingers onto the wire rack to completely cool before serving.

Chocolate Chip Cookie

Prep time: 15 minutes | Cook time: 12 minutes | Serves 6

- 118g butter, softened
- 118g sugar
- 118g brown sugar
- 1 egg
- 1 teaspoon vanilla
- ½ teaspoons baking soda
- ¼ teaspoons salt
- 354g all-purpose flour
- 236g chocolate chips

1. Grease the sheet pan with cooking spray.
2. Beat butter with sugar and brown sugar in a mixing bowl.
3. Stir in vanilla, egg, salt, flour, and baking soda, then mix well.
4. Fold in chocolate chips, then knead this dough a bit.
5. Spread the prepared dough in the prepared sheet pan evenly.
6. Transfer the pan to the Ninja Foodi Digital Air Fry Oven and close the door.
7. Select "Bake" mode by rotating the dial.
8. Press Start/Pause to begin cooking.
9. Serve oven fresh.

Banana Pancakes Dippers

Prep time: 5 minutes | Cook time: 15 minutes |Serves 2

- 225 grams all-purpose flour
- 3 bananas, halved and sliced lengthwise
- 1 tablespoon baking powder
- 1 tablespoon packed brown sugar
- 1 teaspoon salt
- 175 ml whole milk
- 2 large eggs
- 1 teaspoon vanilla extract

1. Combine flour, baking powder, brown sugar, and salt in bowl.
2. Mix the milk and sour cream in a separate bowl, then add the eggs one at a time. Pour in the vanilla extract.
3. Combine the wet and dry ingredients until just mixed.
4. Grease the SearPlate with cooking spray and line it with parchment paper.
5. Select the timer for 16 minutes and the temperature to 190 degrees Celsius.
6. Allow cooling for two minutes before serving.

Easy Carrot Cake

Prep time: 5 minutes | Cook time: 20 minutes |Serves 6

- 1 egg
- 225 grams all-purpose flour
- 1 tsp vanilla extract
- 110 grams sugar
- 7.5 ml (1/2 tbsp) olive oil
- 1 1/2 tsp baking powder
- 1/4 tsp nutmeg
- 1 tsp cinnamon
- 175 grams grated carrots
- 60 ml applesauce
- 1/4 tsp salt

1. Add all ingredients into the mixing bowl and mix until well combined.
2. Pour batter into the greased cake pan.
3. Preheat the oven to 180 degrees Celsius.
4. Select the bake mode, then set the temperature to 180 degrees Celsius and the time for 20 minutes. Press start.
5. Slice and serve.

Cookie Cake

Prep time: 5 minutes | Cook time: 10 minutes |Serves 2

- 115 grams butter, softened
- 100 grams brown sugar, packed
- 50 grams sugar
- 1 egg
- 190 grams all-purpose flour
- 1/2 teaspoon baking soda
- 175 grams semi-sweet chocolate chips

1. Mix the softened butter, brown sugar, and sugar in a large mixing bowl.
2. Mix in the vanilla and egg until everything is well combined.
3. Slowly stir in the flour and baking soda until combined, then stir in the chocolate chips.
4. Spray a 6-inch pan with oil, pour half of the batter into the pan, and press it down to evenly fill it. Refrigerate the other half for later use.
5. Place the pan on a wire rack inside the oven.
6. Select the timer for 5 minutes and the temperature for 190 degrees Celsius.
7. Remove it from the oven and set it aside for 5 minutes to cool.

Cherry Crumble

Prep time: 5 minutes | Cook time: 25 minutes |Serves 8

- 75 grams butter, crumbled
- 450 grams pitted cherries
- 10 tablespoons white sugar
- 2 teaspoons lemon juice
- 150 grams all-purpose baking flour
- 1 teaspoon vanilla powder
- 1 teaspoon ground nutmeg
- 1 teaspoon ground cinnamon

1. oss pitted cherries with lemon juice and 2 tablespoons of sugar in a bowl.
2. Spread the cherry mixture in an 8-inch baking dish.
3. Whisk flour, butter, and 6 tablespoons of sugar in a bowl. Spread this flour mixture on top of the cherries.
4. Mix vanilla powder, nutmeg, cinnamon, and 2 tablespoons of sugar in a bowl.
5. Drizzle this cinnamon mixture on top of the flour mixture.
6. Set its cooking time to 25 minutes and temperature to 165 degrees Celsius, then press "START/PAUSE" to initiate preheating.
7. Serve.

Marinara Sauce

Prep time: 15 Minutes | Cook time: 30 Minutes | Serves 3

- 60 ml extra-virgin olive oil
- 1 small onion, chopped (about 120 ml)
- 3 garlic cloves, minced
- 2 tablespoons minced or puréed sun-dried tomatoes (optional)
- 1 (800-gram) can crushed tomatoes
- 1/2 teaspoon dried oregano
- 1/2 teaspoon dried basil
- 1/4 teaspoon red pepper flakes
- 1 teaspoon kosher salt or 1/2 teaspoon fine salt

1. Place the oil into a medium saucepan over medium heat. When the oil shimmers, add the onion and garlic. Cook, stirring frequently, for 2 to 3 minutes, or until the onion has started to soften bottom of the pot if there is anything stuck. Stir in the oregano, basil, red pepper flakes, and salt.
2. Turn off the heat and let the sauce cool for about 10 minutes. Taste and adjust the seasoning, adding more salt if necessary. Refrigerate in an airtight container for up to a week or freeze for 4 to 6 weeks if not using right away.

Brownie Muffins

Prep time: 5 minutes | Cook time: 10 minutes | Serves 12

- 1 package Betty Crocker fudge brownie mix
- 25 grams walnuts, chopped
- 1 egg
- 80 ml vegetable oil
- 2 teaspoons water

1. Grease 12 muffin molds. Set aside.
2. In a bowl, mix together all the ingredients.
3. Place the mixture into the prepared muffin molds.
4. Press the AIR OVEN MODE button of Ninja Foodi Dual Heat Air Fry Oven and turn the dial to select the "Air Fry" mode.
5. Press the TIME/SLICES button and again turn the dial to set the cooking time to 10 minutes.
6. Now push the TEMP/SHADE button and rotate the dial to set the temperature at 150 degrees Celsius.
7. Press the "Start/Stop" button to start.
8. When the unit beeps to show that it is preheated, open the oven door.
9. Carefully invert the muffins onto the wire rack to completely cool before serving.

Appendix 1 Measurement Conversion Chart

Volume Equivalents (Dry)	
US STANDARD	METRIC (APPROXIMATE)
1/8 teaspoon	0.5 mL
1/4 teaspoon	1 mL
1/2 teaspoon	2 mL
3/4 teaspoon	4 mL
1 teaspoon	5 mL
1 tablespoon	15 mL
1/4 cup	59 mL
1/2 cup	118 mL
3/4 cup	177 mL
1 cup	235 mL
2 cups	475 mL
3 cups	700 mL
4 cups	1 L

Volume Equivalents (Liquid)		
US STANDARD	US STANDARD (OUNCES)	METRIC (APPROXIMATE)
2 tablespoons	1 fl.oz.	30 mL
1/4 cup	2 fl.oz.	60 mL
1/2 cup	4 fl.oz.	120 mL
1 cup	8 fl.oz.	240 mL
1 1/2 cup	12 fl.oz.	355 mL
2 cups or 1 pint	16 fl.oz.	475 mL
4 cups or 1 quart	32 fl.oz.	1 L
1 gallon	128 fl.oz.	4 L

Temperatures Equivalents	
FAHRENHEIT(F)	CELSIUS(C) APPROXIMATE)
225 °F	107 °C
250 °F	120 ° °C
275 °F	135 °C
300 °F	150 °C
325 °F	160 °C
350 °F	180 °C
375 °F	190 °C
400 °F	205 °C
425 °F	220 °C
450 °F	235 °C
475 °F	245 °C
500 °F	260 °C

Weight Equivalents	
US STANDARD	METRIC (APPROXIMATE)
1 ounce	28 g
2 ounces	57 g
5 ounces	142 g
10 ounces	284 g
15 ounces	425 g
16 ounces (1 pound)	455 g
1.5 pounds	680 g
2 pounds	907 g

Appendix 2 The Dirty Dozen and Clean Fifteen

The Environmental Working Group (EWG) is a nonprofit, nonpartisan organization dedicated to protecting human health and the environment Its mission is to empower people to live healthier lives in a healthier environment. This organization publishes an annual list of the twelve kinds of produce, in sequence, that have the highest amount of pesticide residue-the Dirty Dozen-as well as a list of the fifteen kinds ofproduce that have the least amount of pesticide residue-the Clean Fifteen.

THE DIRTY DOZEN

The 2016 Dirty Dozen includes the following produce. These are considered among the year's most important produce to buy organic:

Strawberries	Spinach
Apples	Tomatoes
Nectarines	Bell peppers
Peaches	Cherry tomatoes
Celery	Cucumbers
Grapes	Kale/collard greens
Cherries	Hot peppers

The Dirty Dozen list contains two additional itemskale/collard greens and hot peppers-because they tend to contain trace levels of highly hazardous pesticides.

THE CLEAN FIFTEEN

The least critical to buy organically are the Clean Fifteen list. The following are on the 2016 list:

Avocados	Papayas
Corn	Kiw
Pineapples	Eggplant
Cabbage	Honeydew
Sweet peas	Grapefruit
Onions	Cantaloupe
Asparagus	Cauliflower
Mangos	

Some of the sweet corn sold in the United States are made from genetically engineered (GE) seedstock. Buy organic varieties of these crops to avoid GE produce.

Appendix 3 Index

A

all-purpose flour 9, 13, 18, 22, 27, 36, 57, 58, 59, 60
almond 15
applesauce 59
asparagus 41, 43, 45

B

bacon 19
balsamic vinegar 24, 28, 29, 30, 38
basil 18, 30, 35, 39, 43, 44, 48, 61
bell pepper 25, 31
bread crumbs 17, 44
broccoli 21, 51, 55
brown sugar 12, 13, 20, 52, 57, 58, 59, 60
buns 51
butter 13, 20, 22, 28, 33, 42, 43

C

canola oil 24
cauliflower 51
cayenne 14, 25, 44
Cheddar cheese 10
cheese 9, 10, 11, 12, 14, 15, 17, 18, 19, 20, 21
chocolate chips 58, 60
cinnamon 20, 57, 59, 60
coconut 13
coriander 27, 35, 37
corn 19, 20, 39, 48
cream cheese 18, 19, 34, 49, 57
cumin 14, 19, 27, 37, 55

D

Dijon mustard 33, 43, 46
dried basil 39, 44
dried oregano 18, 24, 26, 38, 39, 42
drumsticks 33
dry mustard 51

E

egg 10, 11, 12, 14, 15, 17, 18, 21, 25

F

fine salt 13, 28, 29, 43
florets 21, 51, 55
flour 9, 13, 17, 18, 22, 27, 28, 35, 36, 38
fresh mushrooms 54
fresh parsley 10, 28, 46, 49

G

garlic 10, 11, 12, 14, 17, 18, 19, 22
garlic powder 10, 11, 12, 17, 19, 22, 34, 41
Greek yogurt 19

H

honey 13, 43

I

Italian sausage 11, 28

J

juice 18, 42, 43, 44, 54, 55

K

kosher salt 12, 13, 14, 20, 22, 27, 28

L

lemon 18, 24, 42, 43, 44, 54, 60
lemon juice 18, 42, 43, 44, 54
lightly beaten 14, 25, 27, 31, 41, 46, 53
lime 42, 54
lime juice 42

M

maple syrup 19, 33, 55
Marinara Sauce 29, 61
mayonnaise 14, 27, 34, 37
milk 12, 13, 15, 22, 26, 28, 36, 55, 57, 59
mozzarella cheese 14, 15, 17, 26, 34, 49
mushrooms 34, 36, 52, 54
mustard 27, 33, 38, 41, 43, 46, 51
mustard powder 38

N

nutmeg 59, 60
Nutritional yeast 17

O

olive oil 13, 14, 18, 20, 24, 26, 28, 30
onion 10, 14, 17, 18, 20, 22, 24, 25, 26, 27, 28
onion powder 10, 17, 22, 24
oregano 18, 22, 24, 26, 38, 39, 42, 61

P

paprika 15, 17, 18, 22, 24, 25, 44, 46, 50, 53
Parmesan cheese 15, 21, 29, 35, 37
parsley 10, 11, 28, 46, 48, 49, 53
pasta 26
pumpkin 9, 19

R

red pepper flakes 61
rice 17, 27, 31, 37, 45, 49, 52, 53

S

salt 9, 10, 11, 12, 13, 14, 15, 17, 18, 19, 20
soy sauce 29, 30, 38, 51
sugar 12, 13, 20, 22, 29, 30, 52, 57, 58, 59

T

thyme 28, 33
tomato 14, 15, 22, 28, 50
tortillas 20, 36, 39

U

unsalted butter 13, 20, 22, 28, 43

V

vegetable oil 13, 22, 27, 28, 36, 37
vinegar 24, 28, 29, 30, 38

W

white wine 43, 44

Y

yogurt 19

Lucy Simmons

Printed in Great Britain
by Amazon